Besch
15 JUL 97
11.99
Barnes + Noble
Lakewood

FROM STALEMATE TO SOULMATE

FROM STALEMATE TO SOULMATE

A GUIDE TO MATURE, COMMITTED, LOVING RELATIONSHIPS

Michael Obsatz, Ph.D.

Augsburg
MINNEAPOLIS

To my wife, Nancy, and my children, Sharyn, Kevin, and Molly.
Thanks for all the love you have brought into my life.

FROM STALEMATE TO SOULMATE
A Guide to Mature, Committed, Loving Relationships

Scripture quotations are from the New Revised Standard Version Bible, copyright © 1989 by the Division of Christian Education of the National Council of the Churches of Christ in the U.S.A. and used by permission.

Cover and book design by Elizabeth Boyce
Cover photo by J. Bonyata and E. Boyce

ISBN 0-8066-2701-8

The paper used in this publication meets the minimum requirements of American National Standard for Information Sciences—Permanence of Paper for Printed Library Materials, ANSI Z329.48-1984. ∞

Manufactured in the U.S.A.   AF 9-2701

01   00   99   98   97   1   2   3   4   5   6   7   8   9   10

CONTENTS

INTRODUCTION: LOVE IS GOD'S GIFT

Love is patient; love is kind; love is not envious or boastful or arrogant or rude. It does not insist on its own way; it is not irritable or resentful; it does not rejoice in wrongdoing, but rejoices in the truth. It bears all things, believes all things, hopes all things, endures all things.

—I CORINTHIANS 13:4-7

A healthy, loving relationship is a sacred gift from God. God wants us to love each other and create together. When God told his people to be fruitful and multiply, he meant for them to create in all kinds of ways—to have children, to create more love, to help others, to use their minds to create new inventions.

We also want to be loved. All of us yearn for emotional and spiritual connectedness. We want to be accepted for who we are. We want to be forgiven for our mistakes and sins. We want affection, understanding, tenderness, and nurturing.

When we are courting and putting on our best face, we often fall in love with love. We may be so overjoyed and infatuated that we minimize the limits of our spouse. He or she may be so taken with us that he or she doesn't comment on our most annoying traits. After a while, after the initial infatuation ends, we are left with a person—whole and holy—but human, nevertheless.

A long-term, committed relationship, a marriage of the body, mind, and soul requires something much more difficult than a courtship. Loving someone forever requires sensitivity,

9

empathy, and generosity—three very mature traits. The real commitment to a meaningful life together takes place after you know who your spouse really is and can accept him or her with strengths and weaknesses alike.

What do we want in a soulmate? We want someone who will love us despite our limits, challenge us to grow, and help us feel connected and sure-footed in a sometimes shaky world. We want to create a home and homelife that is an island of safety and support in a sometimes unsafe world. We want someone who will take a genuine interest in who we are and what we want out of life.

We are enthusiastic about our partner during those first three months. However, after a while, some marriages may grow stale, boring, or unexciting. Rather than openly discussing ideas and issues, the relationship becomes lock in a stalemate. We start to take our spouse for granted. We don't remember anniversaries. We make assumptions without checking them out. We become careless and inconsiderate. We may become bored with our partner when we can almost predict their behavior.

Marriages that often start out with lofty and loving promises may end up boring and lonely. A marriage may be "made in heaven" but it takes earthly work to create a heavenly union.

This book is about working—both on oneself and on the relationship. We assume that, with motivation to grow and a deep desire to spiritually and emotionally nurture your marriage partner, any stale marriage can be refreshed with a spiritual and emotional tune-up.

This book is called *From Stalemate to Soulmate* because it helps one move from a stalemate with one's spouse to having a soulmate. When you have a "soul" connection with your spouse, you share many things. You are both interested in each other's journey, and feel a deep and meaningful connection much of the time.

We are proposing twenty-five ways to keep your love light shining. Instead of discussing what is wrong with women or how men don't get it, we will explore how partners can grow individually and as a couple. We won't focus on women who love too much or men who need too much, or how women and men come from different planets. We are, in fact, on the same planet—God's planet. God has given us skills to create a healthy marriage. If we don't use these skills, we are disappointing ourselves, our spouse, and God.

The process of moving from a marriage that is stale to one that is soul-connected takes time, energy, work, and commitment. As you read the chapters and work on the exercises in this book, you will learn many things about your spouse and yourself that will surprise you. This process may be slow at times and fast at other times. However, if you work diligently, your life will be anything but stale. Most marriages can become deeper and more spiritual, if the spouses are willing to discuss and share their own journeys. The fact that you are reading this may mean that you are ready to listen, speak, pay attention, and grow together. Blessings on your journey! Bon voyage!

HOW TO USE THIS BOOK

The chapters in this book cover topics ranging from simple to complex. Some couples will find certain chapters more complicated due to their own special situation. If a chapter seems too overwhelming or too complex, skip it for now and go on to the next one. Select those sections you are ready to work on. You may take turns selecting which chapter you want to work on. If you can't agree on where to start, select cards with the higher card getting the first pick.

Take time for each of you to read the chapter. Point out some of the highlights of the chapter to each other. See if you both have similar reactions and a similar understanding of the issues discussed. Write your individual answers to the questions, speak them into a tape recorder, or just discuss your answers without writing them down. You may add additional questions that seem to flow out of those already there. Use the chapter questions as a springboard for personal conversation.

The exercises and questions after many of the chapters give you an opportunity to put the ideas discussed into practice. Understanding the issues is the first step. Working on them is the next step. The third step is discussing how you can grow individually and together as you put the ideas into practice.

How long should you give yourselves to get through this book? As long as it takes. Some couples may want to work on a chapter a week. Others may have more time and want to read chapters and do exercises three or four times a week.

Some of the issues may not seem very important to you at this time. Feel free to skip around and work on those that seem most vital. The aim of this book is to facilitate meaningful conversation between the two of you. You will become soulmates as you discuss these issues with honesty, directness, and caring. Soulmates are created when two people are willing to take the time, energy, and personal risks to share their needs, wants, and feelings.

If some of the issues seem too difficult to tackle on your own, you might want to consider professional couple counseling with a therapist or pastor.

THE BASICS

1

REVEALING OURSELVES: FACING THE FEAR OF INTIMACY

Real intimacy is, first and foremost,
a journey into this unknown.
—JOHN WELWOOD, *JOURNEY OF THE HEART*

When we share our lives, our hearts, our souls, our innermost longings with another, we are vulnerable. We open ourselves up emotionally, and risk rejection, disapproval, and abandonment. Loving another person involves risk, and many of us fear being hurt. We may be fearful of being abandoned or rejected. We may be fearful of being criticized, shamed or humiliated. Or, we may be fearful of being smothered or engulfed.

Some of our fears are real, and some are imagined. We can become preoccupied with fears or try to deny that they exist. It is better to be honest and direct in marriage. We need to acknowledge that sometimes we are afraid.

Whenever we reveal ourselves, we take a risk. We wonder, "How will my spouse respond to what I said or did? Will my trust be betrayed? Will my feelings be minimized? Will my spouse get tired of me and leave?" There is a natural fear of being close, vulnerable and trusting. Along with fear comes jealousy and envy. We worry, "Will my spouse find someone better than I?"

It is natural to have fears, and intimate relationships often bring up old, unresolved issues from childhood. In our early years, we were hurt by people on whom we depended. Our parents were imperfect, and at times, they could not be there for us in the way that we needed. So we have leftover feelings related to fear of abandonment and rejection. It is with our spouse that we often feel more safe to be that immature self that we were in childhood.

The first step is to acknowledge that all intimate relationships are scary. In addition to fearing abandonment or rejection, we may fear our spouse becoming ill or dying. The more we love, the more we have to lose. The more open and vulnerable we become, the harder it would be to have the relationship end. Loss comes from attachment to others. Some people are so afraid of loss that they refuse to be vulnerable in relationships. They pretend not to care and avoid becoming emotionally close. Some people disguise their fear by being angry or bitter. Others use sarcasm to distance themselves.

Since all intimate relationships require vulnerability and involve risk, why do we enter into them? We risk because otherwise we would have nothing. Fear, risk, vulnerability, and healthy relationships are inseparable. It is a challenge to let go and be who you really are. It is a challenge to reach out and give of yourself time and time again. Letting another person know who you really are requires a trust that they will take you seriously, hold what you share in confidence, and accept you with your strengths and weaknesses.

The second step is to share your fears with your partner and give each other support and reassurance. Ask your partner to tell you if they feel you are distancing yourself, or controlling, or engulfing. Take your spouse's fears seriously and promise to respect them with the tenderness a good parent gives a child.

The third step is to notice signs of when your spouse may be feeling afraid and ask about it in a gentle way. Listen with an open mind and a willing heart.

The fourth step is to enlist God's love and grace to ease your fears. The spiritual answer to fear is love—love of self, and love of others. On a spiritual level, you are ultimately connected and loved, and you can never lose that love. While in the material world people come and go, the spiritual connection is everlasting. You may chose to pray when afraid. You may read the Bible. You may choose to go to a quiet place and meditate. The Bible reminds us that fear is not the last word, love is.

The purpose of loving another is not only to be loved back. It is also to reflect God's love for us out into the world. Loving others without expecting anything in return is the ultimate kind of love, and you will spiritually grow as you love in this way.

MOVING INTO ACTION

Write and describe each of these fears on a sheet of paper.

1. Fear of abandonment

2. Fear of rejection

3. Fear of shame or humiliation

4. Fear of being smothered or engulfed

5. Fear of having spouse become ill or die

In describing each fear, write about when it comes into your awareness, how you experience it, and the behaviors that result. Write about how your spouse can be helpful when each of these fears arise. What kind of reassurance or support do you need? Is it verbal or physical?

Share your writing with your spouse and discuss how you experience your fears in different ways.

Create a prayer that affirms your ability to overcome your fears together.

Here are some questions to discuss:

1. What do we fear the most?

2. What behavior from our partner triggers our fears?

3. What are we holding back in our marriage relationship due to fear?

4. What kind of reassurance and support do we need when we share our deepest selves with each other?

5. What have we done recently that has encouraged more sharing, more openness, more trust?

6. Are there any childhood memories that tend to keep us stuck in fear?

7. Is there any therapeutic work that can be done to move out of fear?

8. How can prayer, Bible reading or spiritual support help us turn our fears into love?

There is no fear in love, but perfect love casts out fear.
—1 JOHN 4:18

2
BEING THERE

Mature love brings with it the promise of abundance—a realiza-
tion that our lives are more full, more connected and more empow-
ered than ever before. Through this celebration of connection we
learn to take pride in the "we" that we have become.
—LARRY A. BUGEN, *LOVE AND RENEWAL*

There is something unique about being the most special person in another person's life. Couples who want to thrive together for a lifetime need to believe that their relationship is unlike any other that their spouse has. It has a sexual component, and that makes it unique. It also must have a sense of "we-ness," an acknowledgment that says to the world, "We are a team, a united front. We are committed. What we share is different from what we share with anyone else." Both partners need to place a priority on the relationship and have a special and unique role in their spouse's life. Being with each other, listening, sharing, and spending a quantity of quality time contributes to this relationship's specialness.

A couple, Tom and Martha, have become so involved in their own worlds that they hardly spend any time together. Tom is a sales manager, and Martha designs sets for a theater production company. Their jobs require that he work long days and she work long evenings. They rarely eat together or spend meaningful time together. They have developed other close friendships and look to those people for support and validation. As a result, Tom and Martha are unsure of their marriage and what it means to them.

In addition to being together, partners need to feel valued for who they are and feel they are fairly treated. In American society, gender roles can create tension between men and women. Boys and girls are socialized to act differently and are, in some cases, antagonistic to each other. Men are offered certain political and economic advantages. Women are allowed to express more feelings. Men receive more freedom in the outer world. Women receive more freedom in the inner world. Boys are taught not to cry. Girls soon learn that there have been no women presidents. Inequalities that exist between men and women can cause tension, stress, and resentment.

It is important in a healthy marriage to bridge the gender gap by having both partners support and validate each other. Spouses need to feel of equal worth in each other's eyes.

Being equals does not mean being or doing the same things. It means that each spouse feels valued and believes that he or she has choices about how to act in situations. Partnership involves teaching and learning as each partner learns what life means to someone of the other gender.

It seems obvious that being there physically is required for a long-term committed marriage. Tom and Martha had to learn that if they wanted their marriage to thrive, they needed to carve out time to spend together. But beyond that, they needed to learn what the other felt about important issues in their lives. Physical and emotional presence of mind and feelings are necessary. To provide this, each spouse has to empathize and imagine what it would be like to be the other spouse. A man needs to ask himself: "How would I feel about this if I were in her shoes?" A woman needs to empathize with life's struggles from her husband's perspective.

Many couples that I counsel complain that one partner seems preoccupied, aloof, or just not involved. Being there emotionally requires active listening, eye contact, and constructive feedback. This is more than parroting back, "I hear what you are saying." Genuine presence is shown through body language and patience. This means that one doesn't try to hurry the other into simple conclusions or solutions. Telling the details of one's own life story takes time. It helps to set aside a period of time when interpersonal communication becomes the major focus rather than the backdrop for television watching, dealing with children, or reading the newspaper.

Without a commitment of time, couples drift apart, become immersed in their own battles and journeys, and lose touch with each other. Paying attention to the subtleties of communication shows your spouse that you really do care, this very minute. Focused attention requires putting other thoughts and feelings out of your mind temporarily. Let your spouse know you are interested, motivated to help, and really listening. Ask your spouse what he or she needs from you when you talk. Ask: "Do you want me to just listen? Do you want suggestions? Do you want support?"

Doing this allows the person speaking to think about their own expectations of their spouse. Why am I telling you this? What do I need from you as I deal with this particular issue?

MOVING INTO ACTION

Spend ten minutes just being with your spouse. Let your spouse talk while you just listen. Pay attention, show interest without interrupting.

With your spouse, spend ten minutes writing down some of the current concerns you have and some current concerns you think your spouse has.

After you have written, compare answers with your spouse. Did your partner know what was going on in your life? Did you know what was foremost in your spouse's mind?

Write out your answers to the following questions and then discuss each one with your spouse:

1. How much time during the week do we spend focusing on each other and the relationship?

2. How well do I listen to my partner?

3. What do I need to do to improve my attentiveness to my spouse?

4. How does our sense of "we-ness" get communicated to ourselves, our children, or our friends?

5. How do we give each other the sense that our relationship is a priority?

6. Do we each treat each other as equals?

7. Are there any areas where we experience unfair or unequal treatment by our spouse?

8. What do we need to do to change this?

9. In what ways do we show that we appreciate and value each other for what we do?

Listen to me and be attentive to the words of my mouth.
—PROVERBS 7:24

3
CODEPENDENCY AND INTERDEPENDENCY

When one loves, there is a new delight in being alive, new powers of awareness, of perception. . . . Ordinary tasks are elevated; simple events are sacramentalized. Persons are born again, regain an innocence and a purity and a wholeness. They experience physical exhilaration, a propensity for play. . . . New powers sprout, new confidence is gained. Projects are conceived, a community is born, a heritage is transmitted. Love conspires and collaborates and is fruitful. There is a glimpse of self-transcendence. . . . "
—JOAN PULS, *A SPIRITUALITY OF COMPASSION*

Melodie Beattie, in *Codependent No More*, states that many people live in codependent relationships. According to her, codependency is an unhealthy connection in which people desperately need their partner in order to feel good about themselves. Codependent people cling, nag, blame, and demand. A person in such a relationship cannot live without the other person and defines himself or herself totally by the relationship. Frequently, people who are in codependent relationships have no friendships or interests outside the relationship. They live in desperate fear that they are worthless and unlovable. They try to control their partner, out of fear of losing them.

The amount of writing about this concept has made some people wonder about the health of their marriages. When we love someone, don't we need them? Don't we sometimes feel lonely or empty when they are gone?

In contrast to a codependent relationship, a relationship is healthy when it is interdependent, when both people feel a sense of equality, connection, and value for who they are. In an interdependent relationship, both people feel free to lean and be leaned on, and to learn from each other. One may sacrifice for one's spouse out of love, but it is not done out of fear that one's spouse will leave. Sacrifice is part of compromise, and compromise is part of interdependency. Healthy interdependent marriages require that both spouses sacrifice at times, but neither should be in control of the other.

Both partners know they are loved by God, and that love allows them to accept themselves and their partner as fallible human beings. Christians believe that God's grace has been revealed especially in the life of Jesus Christ. In an unpublished paper, the Reverend Charles Lodgson Christopher identifies four aspects of grace:

1. Life is good and can be responded to with trust.
2. You are accepted. You are fundamentally all right as you are, with all of your limits and possibilities.
3. The past is forgiven. Liberating grace frees you from the weight of the past.
4. The future is open. You can go forward from here and make decisions. Anything is possible with God's love and grace.

This grace affirms that we are lovable and accepted, with our limits, faults, and self-centeredness. With each partner sure of his or her lovability, he or she can give to the other, sacrifice at times, and be content to not always have his or her own way. Interdependent, mature love is based on mutual trust and a willingness to give and take.

Couples who share an interdependent life take pride in each other's accomplishments. They show respect for each other and try to avoid put-downs or petty criticisms. When they give each other feedback, it done out of love, for constructive ends.

There are times when each person feels small, scared, or childlike. Interdependent relationships allow for partners to take turns nurturing and being nurtured. The most important aspects of healthy, interdependent relationships are:
— Generosity is encouraged for both spouses
— Each partner feels loved and valued
— Both can be strong and weak
— Sacrifices are made for the sake of the other, not out of guilt but out of love
— Both feel equally respected

This mature love brings an excitement about being alive and many new possibilities.

MOVING INTO ACTION

Identify several situations in which you have sacrificed for your spouse or your spouse has sacrificed for you.

1. Discuss why you each of you did what you did, and how it felt.

2. Consider what God's grace means in your life. Create a prayer of thanksgiving for that grace and commit to praying it daily.

3. Are you each capable of leaning and being leaned on? When and how has that occurred?

For by grace you have been saved through faith, and this is not your own doing; it is the gift of God.
—EPHESIANS 2:8

4
LEARNING TO KNOW AND LOVE OURSELVES

*The great paradox of love is that it calls on us to be fully
ourselves and honor our individual truth, while also letting
go of self-centeredness, and giving without holding back. . . .
Thus being genuinely present and intimate with another person
forces us to live on the edge of the unknown. Here we are also
on our growing edge, where old, familiar ways of being leave
off and new possibilities keep opening up before us.*
—JOHN WELWOOD, *JOURNEY OF THE HEART*

What does it mean to be fully ourselves? Some authors insist
that being in a loving relationship forces people to face themselves. It is through the supportive feedback from one who
cares that we learn about our strengths, weaknesses, limitations, goals, dreams, needs, and feelings.

Many people haven't thought much about who they are.
They become so busy with day-to-day living that they don't
reflect very often. We can go through years of schooling and
learning about science, math, and literature and yet learn very
little about ourselves. Where do we begin?

You were born with certain genetic traits and characteristics. Some of these include temperament, intelligence, and
physical capabilities. Through the years you can learn and
grow and change some of these characteristics. In other
words, if you tend to be quick-tempered, you can alter that
through breathing, taking time outs, and controlling your

impulses. While you cannot change your physical size, you can change your athletic capabilities by practicing. Intelligence can be modified through reading and other types of intellectual stimulation.

When we ask, *Who are you?*, we may be asking about your needs, feelings, goals, or dreams. Some people answer with their profession. Other people may say they are Lutheran or Methodist or Episcopalian. Their religion helps define their values, and hence, who they consider themselves to be.

Still others respond with their political leaning, or their marital status, or their stage in life. In truth, we are many things, and we are always changing. Self-understanding and self-awareness involve a knowledge of your feelings and moods, your goals and dreams, and your sense of identity. The more you know about yourself, the more you are capable of understanding your spouse at a deep level.

After you become familiar with your needs, feelings, and goals, you can think about self-acceptance. Do you accept and love yourself for who and what you are—right now? Some people believe it is selfish to love oneself. Other people believe that all love ultimately comes from self-love directed outward. If one doesn't love oneself, how can one possibly love others?

Loving yourself is knowing that God's grace surrounds you, and what God loves is definitely lovable. This means that you need to accept your faults and limits and work on being the best you can be but still love yourself where you are now.

Some people show that they love themselves by being patient with themselves when they make a mistake. You may not always like what you do, but you can still love your inner core or essence. There may be things about yourself that you really want to change. This doesn't mean you can't love yourself while you are trying to change. You may not like every aspect of yourself—but you can still love the being that you are.

Self-acceptance can give a person a sense of inner peace. It allows us to accept the shortcomings of others and see their inner beauty even when they do something that displeases us. Self-acceptance is a cornerstone of a happy and healthy marriage. It provides the stability in a life that will go through many changes.

Sometimes people are more able to love themselves when they feel affirmed by their partner. It works both ways. Self-affirmation encourages one to accept one's spouse, and love from a spouse encourages self-affirmation.

MOVING INTO ACTION

The first question to ask yourself is about your journey. You have come from somewhere, you are somewhere, and you are going somewhere. Where do you want your life to head? What do you want to accomplish? What does your spouse want to accomplish? Why is this important to you?

1. What are your most predominant moods, and how do you feel about those moods?

2. What makes you happy, sad, disappointed, angry?

3. What are your strengths and weaknesses?

4. What are you trying to change?

5. What do you need from your partner, from your work, from your friends?

6. Do you accept and affirm yourself for who you are?

7. Do you forgive yourself for your limits, mistakes, and weaknesses?

8. What keeps you from loving yourself more? How can you change this?

Share these responses with your spouse, and listen to his or her responses. Discuss these questions:

1. What goals, dreams, and ideas do you have in common?

2. What are some new things you have learned about yourself and each other answering these questions?

Beloved, let us love one another, because love is from God; everyone who loves is born of God and knows God.

—1 JOHN 4:7

5
SEEING THE BIG PICTURE

For everything there is a season,
and a time for every matter under heaven.
—ECCLESIASTES 3:1

Some of us become so immersed in the current details of our lives that we don't see very far ahead. Living with another person for forty or fifty years requires being able to be here now, in the moment, but also being able to develop a sense of perspective about life. This long-term view means that we see daily events in terms of future consequences. We begin to understand that over the course of life people have ups and downs. Life consists of health, illness, love, disappointments, betrayals, accidents, joyous times and celebrations, losses, renewals, and backsliding. Once we understand the complexity of the life cycle, we can realize that there is more to each of life's events than we see in the present moment.

The meaning of some of the events in our lives often does not become clear until later. What seems like a catastrophe can become a blessing, an opportunity, a godsend. Small moments add up to larger weeks, and it is important not to judge ourselves, each other, or life too harshly on the basis of a current feeling or situation.

God has not yet revealed everything to us. Only gradually, slowly, can we begin to discern the complexity of our lives. God is not finished with us yet. That is why some people suggest that we "go with the flow" or "trust the process." A partner's idiosyncrasies matter less over a lifespan. Part of learning to live with another person and accept him or her as is, is learning to cherish your partner's gifts more than resenting his or her faults. Life is life. A marriage is a marriage. It will have its times of closeness and its times of distance. We will feel differently about it at various times in our lives.

When you can see a relationship in perspective, over the long haul, you realize that it will go through changes, stages, and transformations. It is a journey, a mystery, to be traveling through life with someone else. The current bumps are a little easier to take when you can see that all roadways have their dips and potholes. Life is not smooth, and our individual and joint journeys are not smooth either.

Our life together is like a concert. Some pieces will be more appealing to us than others. Sometimes the rhythm will be off. Some instruments will play out of time. Sometimes the timing is wrong. Still, the concert will be a concert.

Seeing the larger picture, seeing life and relationships in perspective, allows us to let go, forgive, and accept each other. We don't overreact to small events because over the long haul they are not worth getting upset about. Having a larger vision allows us to separate the vital issues that must be dealt with from those that are less important and can be left alone.

MOVING INTO ACTION

Take thirty minutes, write answers to these questions, and discuss your responses together. Imagine that you are celebrating your 50th wedding anniversary together. Look back at your marriage.

1. What are some of the major accomplishments you will have shared together?

2. What have been some of the most difficult hurdles that you will have jumped over together with each other's support?

3. What are some things you have worried or argued about that were not very important when you look at the larger picture?

4. Consider the amount of time you spend discussing, arguing, and or thinking about the "small stuff." What do you want to do about that?

For now we see in a mirror, dimly, but then we will see face to face. Now I know only in part; then I will know fully, even as I have been fully known.
—1 CORINTHIANS 13:12

SHAPING HEALTHY
RELATIONSHIPS

6

TRUSTING YOUR PARTNER, GOD, AND LIFE

*We need to trust each other so much because we give each
other so much. Think of commitment as a gift—the gift of one
self to another. . . . We give a big chunk of ourselves, the most
vulnerable part, the part that gets hurt badly if it is let down or
betrayed. And trust is the only way we have of coping with
the risk of such extravagant giving. . . . We need to trust someone
to care for us during the low ebbs, when life's energy bottoms
out, and we are too weak, too tired to take care of ourself.*
—LEWIS B. SMEDES, *CARING AND COMMITMENT*

Ron and Norma are newly married. They have both been
divorced and have had negative experiences with their previ-
ous partners. When Ron is asked to help a female fellow
employee do some construction on her house, Norma is
angry. "Why would you agree to spend three whole weekends
over at her house? You know she is interested in you, and she
doesn't like me. She has never acknowledged our marriage,"
she tells him. Norma is clearly suspicious of Ron's friend's
motivation. She resents the amount of time Ron would spend
away from her with another woman. She is fearful that she
might lose Ron. She is unsure of the commitment they made
to each other.

Trust is probably the most basic need in a relationship.
Learning to trust, building trust, and being trustworthy are
complicated issues. Trust involves keeping the relationship

special and unique, being consistent, and believing in your partner. Trusting your spouse means having faith that he or she is reliable and honest.

Another issue related to trust is abandonment. Because we all fear abandonment to some degree, we want a partner on whom we can depend. The way to develop trust in a relationship is to ask directly for what you want and to be explicit about your expectations. Spouses develop trust over time by demonstrating that they care, mean what they say, and will do what they promise. Commitment is intertwined with trust. A committed relationship requires that each spouse respect the other's privacy, maintain confidentiality about shared information, and take the other seriously.

Partners learn to trust each other with their very lives. They live together, drive together, and often have children together. They care for each other in sickness and at times of sadness, loss, and disappointment. Spouses want to be loved for who they are, deep down, if even their physical appearance changes. They must trust that their partner will be careful with their possessions, feelings, and reputation.

Relationships that lack trust are filled with hostility, fear, and resentment. When trust is betrayed, it shakes the very foundation of a relationship. Some people have been hurt so badly in the past that they have vowed never to trust again. Learning to trust again after past betrayals can be a slow process. But trust can and does grow over time, as spouses feel, deep in their souls, that their partner is responsible, consistent, committed, and truly caring.

An important aspect of trust is setting clear boundaries. Both partners should be clear about their limits, their desire for privacy, and how they expect their bodies to be treated. Setting clear boundaries and discussing them means that each partner is aware of what is important to other. Boundary violations rarely occur when each partner is respectful of the other.

With regard to spiritual trust, Christina Baldwin maintains that "fear is generated by trying to impose order or control on things we do not have control over. Life is in control, but not in *our* control." Along with trust in our spouse, healthy marriages involve spiritual trust—belief that God is there, life is good, and we will receive what we need. Trusting in the love of God allows us the generosity to trust our partner. Knowing God loves us helps us feel lovable, so we are not threatened when our spouse has close friendships with others.

Spiritual trust involves the belief that we will make it through the hard times, with our help, our spouse's help, and God's help. Spiritual trust is a cornerstone of a healthy marriage. God's grace toward us spares us from fearing that we are unworthy of love. God's grace toward us gives us the freedom to love our spouse with all of our heart and soul.

We trust that we will be cared for. We trust that we will not be abandoned by our spouse and by God. We trust that no matter what happens, we will cope and flourish. This basic belief in the goodness of life provides the foundation for trust in marriage—being able to let go, being able to forgive, and being able to accept the joys and sorrows that come our way.

MOVING INTO ACTION

Write the word "trust" on a piece of paper. Then write all the words that come to mind when you think about trust. Write about your trusting God and how God has provided what you need in the past. Write about what trust means in your marriage. Share your ideas with your spouse and discuss the following questions:

1. What can I do to increase the trust in my marriage?

2. What clear boundaries can I set that will insure that I will be respected and supported?

3. What can I do to develop more trust in God and in the goodness of life?

Try the trust walk, an exercise that is done with one partner leading his or her blindfolded spouse on a walk for fifteen minutes. The leader sees to it that his or her spouse does not run into anything during this walk. After you have taken roles both as leader and blindfolded follower, discuss how the experience felt to you.

Trust in the Lord, and do good; so you will live
in the land and enjoy security.
—PSALM 37:3

7

LEARNING FROM
AND APPRECIATING
ONE ANOTHER

When two people create a path together, it is as though their individual intelligence and wisdom join together in a synergistic way, acting as a larger, guiding force that can show them each where they most need to grow. . . . When two partners appreciate that their connection invariably points them in the direction of growth, they can begin to regard any situation that comes up in their relationship as a teacher.
—JOHN WELWOOD, *JOURNEY OF THE HEART*

Partners who wish to grow old together need to teach one another and be open to learning from each other. Each of us has unique talents and skills. Each of us also has blind spots that keep us stuck. The marital team has the incredible opportunity of learning from and teaching one another.

By working as a team, spouses can avoid feeling in competition with one another. They can cooperatively share knowledge so each one benefits from the wisdom of the other. The challenge is to be a patient teacher and a willing learner. It is important to see the process as give-and-take, with neither spouse being superior to the other. Pushing something on someone will not work. Spouses need to be ready to learn, and willing to express their desire to learn.

In addition to teaching skills, we can teach our partner new beliefs, values, and attitudes. We can learn from just observing each other if we do so without judgment or fear. If every situation is viewed as a opportunity to learn and grow, the marital journey is one of increasing awareness, personal growth, and maturity.

John is very organized. His wife, Jennifer's style is a less structured. John focuses on logic for learning. Jennifer is intuitive. Jennifer can learn some logical reasoning skills from John, and John can learn how to trust his intuition more from Jennifer. Neither way is right or wrong. Both can be helpful, depending on the situation.

Some partners have good long-term memories. Others have incredibly outgoing personalities. Still others are excellent with finances and computers. There is no end to what we can learn, and marriage gives us a wonderful opportunity to pick up skills from our partner.

Rather than see our partner's differences as threatening, we can learn to value what they have and try to learn from them. Spouses want to be acknowledged for their skills and for who they are as people. Because we go through life being ignored by many people, it is important that the one person nearest and dearest to us pay attention to us and value us for who we are. Verbalizing affection, giving positive feedback, and being grateful are part of a spiritual attitude called "the attitude of gratitude."

Tom told Susan that he loved her, but he never came right out and told her how much he enjoyed her sparkling personality and friendly laugh. As a result, Susan didn't know what he liked about her. When she asked him directly, he said, "Of course, I think you're wonderful. I love your smile and your laugh." He didn't realize that she needed him to verbally express his appreciation.

Being grateful for one's blessings means thanking God for all the good things we have in our lives. It means acknowledging that even some of the difficult challenges bring us greater awareness and break down illusions. We grow from adversity, and we receive many blessings.

Marriage is indeed a sacred union, and we are blessed to have someone who will be with us through the days of our lives. Your partner has given his or her self to you. He or she loves you, with your limits and faults. Having an attitude of gratitude means noticing the skills and talents of your partner and letting him or her know how wonderful they are and how much you appreciate them.

MOVING INTO ACTION

Think about and list some of your own and your spouses's skills, attitudes, beliefs, and talents.

1. Have you taught any of these to your partner?

2. What have you learned from your partner? Discuss your lists together. Remember to appreciate your partner for what he or she has taught you and for his or her willingness to learn from you. Express your appreciation.

3. Identify something that each of you would like to teach the other. Set a date and time. After you have learned what the other has taught, discuss how the entire teaching/learning process went.

4. What else would you like to learn from your spouse?

5. What else would you like to teach your spouse that you believe would be helpful to him or her?

6. How could your partner express appreciation in ways that would be most gratifying to you?

Take my yoke upon you, and learn from me; for I am gentle and humble of heart, and you will find rest for your souls.
—MATTHEW 11:29

8
ENJOYING TIME APART

We must possess a willingness and an ability to be alone. For paradoxically, it is from our solitudes that we speak and act effectively. Our truest words are born in silence. Our inner resources become the gift we lay at the feet of community. Only in recovering our deepest selves can we communicate freedom and wholeness to others.
—JOAN PULS, *A SPIRITUALITY OF COMPASSION*

While time together is important and necessary in building a strong, healthy relationship, time apart is also vital because it allows each of you to connect with yourselves and with God. Time alone can give you a chance for meditation, prayer, reflection, integration of ideas, getting in touch with feelings, and counting your blessings.

Jesus knew the value of time apart and spent many hours in solitude in the desert, on a mountaintop, in a garden. Often such a natural setting provides us with opportunities for inspiration, insight, and opportunities for healing.

A healthy partnership builds in time for solitude, peace, and revitalization. It may be a hot bubble bath, a long bike ride, a drive in the country, a quiet walk in the woods, or a visit to a retreat center or church. There are streams, ponds, and rivers for those who find water refreshing and beautiful. Even though there may be crowds of shoppers, some people enjoy wandering alone in shopping malls where they feel that they are anonymous and can delve into their own thoughts and feelings. Some folks like to tinker in their workshops or garages. Movies can provide diversion and space for alone time.

We have our special places from the past—those valuable sanctuaries where we felt safe and secure. We also have special places that we have recently discovered—places where we feel nurtured and gain insights. Wherever you can find peace, sanctuary, and renewal, that is where you need to spend some of your time alone.

There are people who are fearful of being alone. They are reminded of those lonely Saturday nights during their adolescence or early adulthood when they lacked a special date. For others, the time to think and examine their lives may be frightening. In time alone, people can realize certain losses or disappointments they may have been denying while being too pre-occupied or busy. Being alone may provide the opportunity to ask the "ultimate questions" for which they find no answers.

Quiet, meditative experiences can help us focus on our thoughts, goals, and our sense of purpose. Part of becoming soulmates is to discover one's own unique purpose, the reason God created you. Everyone has a unique mission to accomplish on earth. Everyone has special gifts and talents that can be used to enrich others and create more peace and harmony in the world. The more in touch you are with your divine gifts, the more you have to share with your spouse. A friend of mine, Karen, loves to go to the mountains for a few days to be alone. She sits quietly and asks those important questions—Where is my life going? What do I want to do next?

Scheduling time apart can be difficult for couples who have small children and busy lives. Like many of the couples I see in counseling, Frank and Lisa claimed to have no time to spend getting in touch with God, nature, themselves, and life's important questions. They said that earning a living, taking care of the children, and household maintenance filled all their time. However, I pointed out to them that if they spent some worthwhile time away, they may come home more refreshed and energized, and be more efficient in doing their daily tasks. Frank took a bunch of books with him to a friend's cabin. Later in the month, Lisa went to a spirituality retreat farm where she strolled in the woods and journaled about her thoughts and feelings.

They both found the experience so valuable that it is now a regular part of their married life

Not everyone likes time alone. Some people get recharged by spending time with people, while others need a quiet getaway to feel reenergized. This is an area in which couples can negotiate and give each other the freedom they need to find time apart that fits their individual needs.

Taking time to just be—and stop doing for a while is a part of spiritual growth. Some people need a week. Others need just a few hours. While you can experience God's incredible love and grace while you are busy, you can truly know you are loved for being just who you are when you are outwardly doing nothing. Reflection and soul-searching may appear to be invisible, but both may produce visible results.

MOVING INTO ACTION

Plan some time alone this week—even if it is just a few hours. Take a quiet walk by yourself. Let your mind wander.

Plan how you will report what you learned to your spouse. Use some of your alone time to count your blessings. Make a list of all the wonderful things in your life. Discuss the answers to these questions with your spouse.

1. When is the last time you really spent time alone?

2. What did you do? What did you learn from it?

3. Where do you feel most connected to yourself and God?

4. Are there any fears that might keep you from spending time alone?

5. What excuses do you use to keep from spending time alone?

6. Where will you go and when? What will you do?

*Come away to a deserted place all by yourselves
and rest a while.*
—MARK 6:31

9

EMPOWERING
YOUR SPOUSE

*A marriage is God's gift to a man and woman. It is a gift that
should then be given back to Him. A man's wife is literally God's
gift to him. A woman's husband is God's gift to her. But God only
gives gifts that are meant for everyone. So it is that a marriage is
meant to be a blessing on the world, because it is a context in which
two people might become more than they have been alone.*
—MARIANNE WILLIAMSON, *A RETURN TO LOVE*

Because you love and care about your spouse, your spouse
may be more open to learning from you than from anyone
else. When a person is empowered, they feel strong, confident,
and true to themselves. People feel a sense of empowerment
when they believe they can make a difference in the world.

Sonia did not have much confidence in her ability to speak
in front of a group. Ken, her husband, encouraged her to take
the public speaking class that he had taken. He thought she
would benefit from the experience and conquer some of her
fears. Sonia took the course, and it opened a whole new
world for her.

You can empower your partner by the following:
- — Help teach your partner new skills.
- — Open your partner to new ways of thinking.
- — Creative a loving, supportive environment.
- — Affirm your partner's uniqueness and many wonderful qualities.
- — Help your partner with problem-solving options and alternatives.

— Through feedback, help your partner focus on his or her unique purpose for living.

— Help your partner create goals and strategies for attaining those goals.

— Encourage your partner's faith and hope.

— Help your partner set appropriate boundaries, and respect those boundaries.

Spouses can help each other form meaningful friendships. They can encourage each other to take time to get to know and enjoy their friendships.

You can also support each other in your careers. Each person has vocational aspirations and dreams. Partners need to pay attention to each other as they share their work experiences and work hassles. Both partners need to encourage their spouse to do their best and celebrate each other's successes. Both need to be there when their spouse has had a work setback.

Partners can help each other relieve stress from work and give each other helpful suggestions for coping with burnout. You can attend social functions that are sponsored by the workplace and be a supportive presence and cordial guest. Spouses need to balance work and play, career and family life. Each needs the help of the other to achieve healthy balance.

Another type of empowerment is to help your spouse live a healthy life—to eat well and receive enough rest and exercise. You empower your spouse by encouraging them to have meaningful relationships with their friends and family. You empower them by being there in the difficult times, with comfort, support, and reassurance.

You can empower your spouse by having a comfortable place to live, and by keeping it reasonably repaired and clean. You can empower your spouse by pointing out options they have when they don't see obvious choices. Sometimes when one is totally immersed in a situation, one develops tunnel vision. A partner with a different perspective can be very helpful.

Empowerment is very necessary in times of stress, discomfort, loss, and crisis. Spouses need ongoing support and encouragement to help them cope, to help them overcome obstacles, and to give them hope. To nurture each other's growth, spouses need to be present, willing to listen, and willing to help.

MOVING INTO ACTION

Think about the importance of confidence and empowerment in your relationship with your spouse.

1. List of all the ways in which your spouse empowers you.

2. List all the ways you empower your partner.

3. Focus on career goals and aspirations, but also other types of goals related to relationships, hobbies, creativity, learning, and spiritual growth.

4. Discuss your lists together.

5. Are there any additional ways you or your spouse could be more supportive of each other's growth?

Encourage one another and build up each other.
—1 THESSALONIANS 5:11

SKILLS EVERY
COUPLE NEEDS

10
EFFECTIVE
COMMUNICATION

When both partners really want to learn about themselves and each other, the process we call exploration can begin. An exploration is simply spending time talking to each other about things that matter. . . . With a partner who accepts and cares about us, buried feelings can surface. . . . When protected, we are defensive and battle to win, or at least not lose. Working on a relationship often means working on protections rather than just on issues.
—JORDAN AND MARGARET PAUL,
DO I HAVE TO GIVE UP ME TO BE LOVED BY YOU?

He just doesn't talk to me" is a common complaint I hear in counseling sessions. Effective communication is vital for a trusting, mature relationship. There needs to be effective communication about the following aspects of living:

1. Long-range plans, hopes, and dreams
2. Daily maintenance issues (how things get done)
3. Individuals' reactions to their day, job, friendships, extended family
4. Current needs and wishes
5. The importance of the marriage
6. Spiritual issues and concerns

Couples communicate verbally and nonverbally through gestures, tone of voice, physical closeness. Whether communication is verbal or nonverbal, it is important to make sure that the message that is sent is the same as what is received. Joan was angry about something that her husband, Leroy, had said thirty years ago. When we discussed it recently, Joan learned that she had misinterpreted Leroy, and he wasn't saying what she thought he had said. As a result of not checking out the *meaning* of the communication, Joan has been carrying around anger for thirty years.

Effective communication means finding the time to share thoughts and feelings. It means speaking and listening and letting your spouse know they have been understood. It requires giving and receiving feedback. Sometimes it is helpful to repeat back what you thought your spouse said to see if it was accurate.

Another helpful approach is to ask your spouse what kind of response he or she wants. In one situation, a spouse might like their partner to just listen quietly. In another situation, a spouse might prefer reactions and suggestions. In a third situation, your partner may want reassurance and comfort. It is important not to guess what your spouse wants. Ask, and try to give, what your partner needs.

Couples need to be clear about their needs and wants, but it is important that they are able to disagree respectfully when there is a difference of opinion. Power struggles create only ill will and resentment.

Sometimes, we need more clarification. We want our spouse to explain in more detail what he or she means. This can be presented in a loving way, or it can come across critically. Tone of voice makes a difference. If at all possible, try not to interrupt. Sometimes individuals just need to vent emotion without needing a response or a solution.

Try to discern the type of sharing going on. Level 1 sharing is just general chitchat. Level 2 sharing is more personal and requires more intent listening. Level 3 sharing means that your spouse is communicating intimate details that might be scary and difficult to reveal.

There are many skills to be learned and practiced. It is helpful to know when to move a conversation from your spouse to yourself. It is important to set clear limits and boundaries about what you are and are not willing to do. Sometimes, it helps to take a time out and postpone the conversation. This may be because of interruptions or other happenings in the family that make effective private listening impossible.

It is helpful to state the purpose of the communication. One might say: "I'd like to talk with you now because I have some thoughts and feelings that I don't quite understand. I think your feedback would be helpful for me." Or, "I'd like to vent some anger about my boss. Would you just listen and then give me support?"

Problems in communication often occur because one of the partners is not really listening. Other problems stem from unclear intentions. Still other problems come from misunderstandings that occur when one partner does not check out the real meaning of their partner's words.

It is important to set up quiet times for important communication. This might be after the children are asleep or on weekends. Whenever the time, focus on listening and understanding your partner as a soulmate.

MOVING INTO ACTION

Tape record yourself speaking. Listen to the tape and notice how clearly you make your points. Do an inventory of your own verbal communication style. Evaluate yourself as a speaker.

1. When you speak, under what circumstances do you want support, feedback, just listening, or suggestions and advice?

Think of a recent time when you communicated with your partner.

2. Were you clear about your goals for the conversation?

3. Did you receive what you needed?

Evaluate yourself as a listener.

4. Do you listen without interrupting?

5. Do you ask relevant questions for clarification?

6. Do you ask your partner about what they want, need, and expect from the communication?

Write answers to these questions, and then discuss them with your spouse:

7. Are there some taboo subjects that neither or you bring up?

8. What are they?

After you have discussed your communication style as a couple, brainstorm some ways that both of you could be more effective communicators with each other.

Let no evil talk come out of your mouths, but only what is useful
for building up, as there is need, so that your words
may give grace to those who hear.
—EPHESIANS 4:29

11
CREATING AND SHARING
YOUR VISION

One of the most powerfully unifying experiences that a family
can have is in creating a family mission statement.
—STEPHEN R. COVEY, *PRINCIPLE-CENTERED LEADERSHIP*

When you think long-term, with larger perspective, you begin to see the importance of developing a personal vision statement and sharing it with your spouse.

If you have a sense of purpose and meaning in your life, you have more than many people. You know what your life is about, what your gifts are, and how you can use them to assist others in the world. Your vision might include your job, or it might be another vocation, a calling for which you are not paid. You might decide that your vision is to create a harmonious community of friends, to organize a shelter for the homeless, to create a retreat center where people get away to renew and refresh themselves, to write a novel, or to fill your backyard with flowers.

If you have a sense of purpose and direction, you are more likely to have long-lasting relationships. The reason for this is that you will then have a sense of yourself and a reason for living. This means that you probably will not expect your partner to make your life worthwhile; your life will already be meaningful.

As a couple, each partner needs to learn how to coordinate his or her own vision with that of his or her partner. Both partners should feel supported as they seek to attain their life's purpose. M. Scott Peck, in *The Road Less Traveled*, says that real love is nurturing the spirituality of your partner. By this, he means that each of us has a need to connect with the Infinite and a desire to experience life on a higher plane. As we love our partner, we encourage their personal, emotional, and spiritual growth. Part of spirituality is having a sense of personal meaning, a reason to live. When we develop our own vision, share that vision with our spouse, learn of our spouse's vision, and then nurture theirs along with our own, we double our joy. Two people journeying on their vision quests can have very interesting dinner conversations.

Couples benefit from communicating about their goals, wants, dreams, hopes, beliefs, and sharing the hows and whys of achieving them. When we share visions, we can also help each other with the inevitable disappointments and road-blocks that fall onto our path. Finding our soul's purpose, and then acting upon it involves hope and fear, trial and error.

If you and your spouse have no interest beyond the daily grind, your lives can become stale and boring after a while. Couples who have similar visions may have more to talk about. If they share parts of a common vision, they will have a greater understanding of each other. Overlapping visions provide reinforcement, more insightful feedback, and opportunities to work together.

In an article called "Birthing Compassion," author Sue Monk Kidd maintains that people move from the "Authentic I" stage to the "Compassionate We" stage. As people mature spiritually, they realize that they can't focus only on their own lives. They begin to care for others and try to make a genuine difference in the world. It is paradoxical that the more we lose ourselves in the quest for creating a better world, the more we find ourselves.

The compassion we crave in relationships revolves around having the motivation to transcend our selfish individual needs. Two self-absorbed individuals do not reach out to each other. To create a vision, a person needs to be quiet, to think, to contemplate, to assess his or her gifts. As you listen inside, you begin to hear what your purpose is.

One of the most detrimental things we do to children and young adults is ignore this concept of the vision quest. Life, for the young, often revolves around doing what others assign them to do and trying to conform. Many young people do not move from the "Authentic I" stage to the "Compassionate We" stage. And yet, healthy relationships rely upon being compassionate—moving beyond oneself, and caring about another. Relationships that are based only on acquiring material possessions and living up to an image grow stale after a short while. What really keeps people together is learning how to define their own purpose and then sharing their purpose with their spouse. If each partner is committed to nurturing the spiritual growth of the other, the relationship can be interesting and dynamic.

MOVING INTO ACTION

Sit quietly and think about your unique strengths and interests. What is God calling you to do? What have you done that has felt so right, so clearly aligned to your very being?

1. As you gain a sense of clarity about your purpose at this point in your life, write it down, and describe how it manifests itself in your daily activities.

2. After you and your spouse complete this exercise, share your results with each other. Discuss how you can both help each other more clearly define your individual purposes and how you may be able to coordinate them and live them out effectively.

3. List three things you can do to help your spouse live a more spiritually purposeful life.

*This one thing I do: forgetting what lies behind and straining
forward to what lies ahead, I press on toward the goal.*
—PHILIPPIANS 3:13-14

12
LEARNING TO
LAUGH AND PLAY

David danced before the Lord with all his might.
—2 SAMUEL 6:14

Life can be difficult and serious. Newspapers and news programs are filled with horror stories about war, crime, and abuse. We live in a violent world. Life has its share of disappointments, accidents, betrayals, illnesses, and losses. We can be so intense and fear-driven that we don't look at the lighter side of life, learn to laugh, dance, play, and experience joy.

We need to be able to laugh at ourselves, at our own egocentric ways, at our own mistakes, and realize that we sometimes do foolish things. Developing a sense of humor and the ability to smile and laugh at ourselves, relieves tension, breaks through boredom, and gives us hope. We need to take the time to feel joy, dance and celebrate our lives with lightheartedness.

An intimate marriage relationship can provide us with the security and comfort we might need to let our hair down, be silly, and be playful. Partners need to reinforce this spirit of playfulness in each other by setting aside time for fun, enjoyment and laughter. For some couples, children keep them playful because children have a way of being lighthearted and silly. For other couples, taking time to read the comics or a funny book can help keep them laughing. Still others prefer to watch a romantic comedy or a funny situation comedy on television. We may play board games. We may go to an amusement park. We may play sports. We may even play a harmless trick on each other on April Fool's Day. Play involves a childlike quality—a spontaneity, an innocence, and a loss of self-consciousness. When we play, we let ourselves be vulnerable and impulsive.

However what seems humorous to one person might not be funny to another. It is important to know your spouse well enough to understand what will genuinely make them laugh. I have seen couples get into arguments when one said something in jest and the other took them too seriously. Sometimes humor can be a mask for hostility. People can be hurt by things that are supposedly said in jest. Be clear about when you want to play, or that you are in fact, joking around.

Sometimes humor is used to avoid a difficult situation. John is always cracking jokes when Myra wants to discuss something serious. This doesn't go over very well with Myra, and she gets mad at John.

It is sometimes helpful to find other couples to play with. One church has road rallies for their couples' group. Once a year, they go on a driving treasure hunt in separate cars, complete with clues, and a real treasure. At a different gathering, these couples bring "white elephant" gifts to a party, and people opening these gifts laugh at how ridiculous they are. They laugh at rubber chickens and ugly lampshades.

God wants us to laugh, to experience joy. Jesus taught using parables that often have surprise endings. Much of spiritual music is uplifting and joyful. Many spiritual institutions offer individual, couple, and family retreats where play is an important aspect of the experience.

Some people spontaneously play. Others need to set aside a time to be lighthearted. Couples can teach each other to have more fun and develop their sense of humor. Timing is very important, and sensitivity to each other's feelings is also crucial. So learn to laugh and play.

MOVING INTO ACTION

Think about different ways in which you and your partner play and laugh together. Make a list of these activities. Discuss them with your spouse.

1. Which types of play are most appealing to you?

2. What are some ways you can bring more laughter and humor into your lives together?

3. Who are the most playful people with whom you spend time?

4. What may be keeping you from playing more often?

Each of you choose one way in the next week that you will play and one way you will play together.

Rejoice in the Lord always; again I will say, Rejoice.
—PHILIPPIANS 4:4

13
RESOLVING CONFLICT
HARMONIOUSLY

If it is peace you want, seek to change yourself, not other people.
It is easier to protect your feet with slippers
than to carpet the whole of the earth.
—ANTHONY DeMELLO

Charles and Amy seem to disagree about most things. Sometimes they argue for hours about messy dresser drawers or Amy's parents. Some relationships are plagued with continuous conflict. Resolving conflict harmoniously takes time, energy, skills, generosity, and a willingness to listen.

Individuals grow up with different messages about conflict. In some families, people love a good fight. In others, people try to avoid conflict at all cost. They may even pretend that there is no conflict when it is obvious to their spouse that a conflict exists. Some couples believe that conflict draws them closer together, while others feel it pushes them further apart.

The challenge for a healthy relationship is to distinguish between what is worth fighting for and what is not. Once you make that distinction, you can put your efforts into resolving the important conflicts and learning to let go of the rest.

Giving in, letting go, and forgiving are all part of healthy conflict resolution. God wants us to have win/win relationships rather than win/lose ones. Because there are no perfect partners and spouses are never identical twins, you're unlikely to find someone who will agree with everything you want. Total agreement all of the time can also lead to boredom, another form of stalemate. Having differing opinions allows you the incredible spiritual opportunity to learn from each other, to learn how to give and take, and to create priorities.

Conflict management is part of the process of developing a healthy, loving relationship. Learning to argue fairly and respectfully is a vital skill. Resolving conflict involves good listening, focusing on the issue at hand, and believing that positive solutions are possible. Both you and your spouse need to feel respected for your opinions, values, and wishes. Both partners need to listen with empathy and without interruption. Many conflicts are resolved through compromising. For example:

1. Because we did it your way last time, can we do it my way this time?
2. On a scale of one to ten, how badly do you want it? If I want my way 4, and you want your way 8, we can do it your way this time. (Remember, you can't always be an 8.)
3. If you want to eat out, and I want to go to a movie, maybe we could find a way to do both.
4. If you like a neat house, and I like a messy house, maybe we could agree that the main living spaces be up to your standards, but my den could be more messy if I agree to keep the door closed.

Conflict resolution requires patience, commitment, and effort. Both of you need to have faith in each other and in the process. Trusting each other means knowing that your spouse is not planning to dominate or manipulate you.

Many couples get into trouble when they go around and around on the same issues and never resolve anything. I know one couple where Ron wants more time together and Sue wants more time alone. They argue incessantly about it—and rarely come to any compromise. Because they have gotten so accustomed to arguing, they spend little quality time together doing anything else.

In some cases, you can agree to disagree. You can have differing ideas and opinions and not have to come to a clear resolution. However, much of the time, issues such as family vacations, who does which chores, and how major purchases are made require agreement.

If you and your spouse believe that both of you are fair, trustworthy, flexible, and open to both points of view, you will be able to resolve most conflicts harmoniously. Being together means sometimes having to go along with your spouse's wishes and put your own on the back burner for now. Ultimately, both of you will have to believe that you will get what you need and that you will be heard and understood.

MOVING INTO ACTION

Here are some questions to ask each other:

1. What are the main unresolved conflicts in our relationship?

2. When we acknowledge these conflicts and work to solve them, in what ways have we made progress?

3. What strategies can we use for working out solutions?

4. Which conflicts are minor and should be let go?

Select an issue that you believe is resolvable, that is still a conflict for both of you. Perhaps each of you will have to name one. Discuss your wants and needs about this issue. Try to work out a win/win compromise that will allow both of you to have something of what you want.

Be angry but do not sin; do not let the sun go down on your anger.
—EPHESIANS 4:26

14
DEVELOPING A
SUPPORT NETWORK

Life has taught us that love does not consist of gazing at each other, but in looking outward together in the same direction.
—ANTOINE DE SAINT-EXUPÉRY, *WIND, SAND AND STARS*

We all want support from others besides our partner. Without friendships, a couple might become too enmeshed and isolated. The marriage relationship should not be the sole refuge of either partner. Each spouse needs to be supportive of their partner's developing healthy friendships with other people. In addition, the partners should find a few couples whom both of them enjoy. They also need to spend time with their close friends while apart.

Sharon and Tim sometimes disagree about how much time she spends with her friend Julie. Sharon tries to explain to Tim that Julie has been her friend for fifteen years, longer than her marriage. Tim thinks that Julie is too dependent on Sharon and could develop other friendships. Julie explains to Tim that she has other friends, but Sharon knows and understands her better than any of them. Julie and Sharon realize that Tim has been feeling left out, and Julie agrees to do more confiding in Tim.

There is no specific rule for how many friendships people should have. However, it is helpful to have some close friends outside of the marriage because the marriage cannot handle all the emotional weight of a couple. There are times when you need a second opinion. There are times when you want a man's point or view, or a woman's. There are times when you need to do social things apart from your spouse and still have a good, intimate connection.

Some people have difficulty when their partner confides in a person of the opposite gender. Insecurities can leap to the fore, and people fear abandonment. You must reassure your spouse that the relationship is a meaningful friendship. It probably helps to meet in public places rather than the home of a friend of the other gender. Clear boundaries need to be set about the limits of friendship, the kinds of touch the friends can share. Trust and communication are crucial as couples choose to spend time with friends outside of their marriage.

We all need people who will celebrate our victories. We want to have people in our lives who will help us solve our problems. We long for people who share our sorrows. We need people who will believe in us when we are having difficulty believing in ourselves. Friendships are of all sorts—from intense to less involved. The challenge is to divide our time between our family, our spouse, and our friends—so that no one feels cheated or deprived. This might mean setting aside limited time for friendships. It might also mean setting aside two hours every other week to visit with a close friend.

Developing strong friendships takes time, energy, and commitment. Spouses can encourage each other to find supportive people. The challenge is to find the energy and time to be a good spouse to your spouse and a good friend to your friends.

MOVING INTO ACTION

Each of you write down a list of your supportive people and examine your list of friendships.

1. What types of friendships are these?

2. What is missing?

3. What kind of support do you receive from each person on your list?

4. How many individual friends are also couple friends?

5. How can you be more supportive of your partner in finding good friends?

Discuss together your individual and couple friends. Decide if you are content with your friends or if either of you feels the need for new friendships. Make a date to get together this week with one special friend. Following this, discuss with your spouse how your time with your friend went.

Bear one another's burdens, and in this way you will fulfill the law of Christ.
—GALATIANS 6:2

15
GRIEVING OUR LOSSES TOGETHER

When we think of loss we think of the loss, through death,
of people we love. But loss is a far more encompassing theme
in our life. For we lose not only through death, but also by leaving
and being left, by changing and letting go and moving on.
And our losses include not only our separations and departures
from those we love, but our conscious and unconscious losses of
romantic dreams, impossible expectations, illusions of
freedom and power, illusions of safety—and the loss of
our own younger self, the self that thought it always would
be unwrinkled and invulnerable and immortal.
—JUDITH VIORST, *NECESSARY LOSSES*

Loss is a part of living. If we are emotionally attached, we experience loss after loss after loss. Many of us have lost family members, parents, friends. We lose jobs, opportunities, valuables. We experience illnesses, accidents, disappointments and betrayals. We all must grieve these losses in our own unique way, and we need support and help as we go through the grieving process.

As partners, we must acknowledge each other's losses and give each other permission to grieve in our own unique styles. Grieving takes time, and healing is often slow. Some losses are never totally accepted, and grieving can become part of a lifestyle. Problems emerge for couples when they don't understand that grieving is a natural process and when they try to fix their partner's grief by saying "just the right words." None of us can fix grief. We all go through it, and we all suffer.

Recognizing the grieving process as healing is very important in a healthy couple relationship. The more you can discuss grief and loss comfortably together, the more supported each of you will feel. The most difficult loss for a couple may be the loss of a child—because this seems so unfair. Because each partner grieves in his or her own way, with a different style and timetable, spouses may feel abandoned during this time. Especially in this situation as in all expriences of grief, it is important to have the support of friends and family.

When Mary's mother died, she spent several weeks grieving with her family in a distant city. Paul, her husband, also felt very close to Mary's mother but had to stay behind so he could work at his job. When she was gone, he felt alone in his grief. While Mary had a great deal of support, Paul's family didn't understand why he was so affected by his mother-in-law's death. So Paul had to share with Mary upon her return that he needed to grieve also, and he valued her support. Mary welcomed the chance to grieve together with Paul, even though she had already gotten much support from her family.

To gain healthy support for grieving, it is important to:
— Acknowledge your own loss.
— Share it with your spouse.
— Ask your partner for what you need—for example, support, holding, listening.
— Be appreciative when your partner is there for you.
— Find other support people who can help you through your grief.
— Acknowledge your partner's loss.
— Be supportive of your spouse's feelings by listening, affirming, holding.
— Don't expect to shorten the grief period by being present.
— Encourage your partner to find others who will support his or her grieving.

— Plan rituals such as a prayer service, visit to a ceme-
tery, or lighting a candle to commemorate losses and
share them together.

MOVING INTO ACTION

Imagine that you have lost someone you love. How do you
feel?

Each of you make a list of the losses you have experienced. List deaths, developmental losses growing up, losses of
objects and possessions, losses of hopes and dreams, losses
due to illness or accidents, disappointments, betrayals, emotional losses—such as loss of security.

Share your list with one another, and discuss the following questions:

1. How could I have supported you better during your
   losses?

2. How did I communicate my losses to you?

3. How do we differ in our grieving styles?

4. What do I need from you when I am grieving?

*I will turn their mourning into joy, I will comfort them,
and give them gladness for sorrow.*
—ISAIAH 31:13

VITAL ISSUES

16
THE SACRED
AND HEALING
POWER OF SEX

Sex shakes us loose from oppositional mind-sets and other mental distractions that keep us from feeling fully awake to the moment. When we experience it in this way—as a way of being present, rather than merely entertained—its sacred power can enter us. The deepest moments of sexual communion are a sacred play of two-in-one. . . . In allowing us to meet and connect beyond our conventional boundaries, sexuality also provides a healing.
—JOHN WELWOOD, JOURNEY OF THE HEART

For a marriage to thrive, partners must develop positive attitudes toward their own and each other's sexuality. Sexual interaction is often a mirror of the other aspects of a couple's intimate relationship. Sensitivity, caring, and responsiveness in intimate communication can also manifest itself in a couple's sexual behavior.

Sex is a God-given gift. It is sacred, wonderful, and life-affirming. A couple that views their sexuality as a holy gift from the Divine can utilize its power to affirm each other and the relationship.

Sexuality is a need, a drive. It can encourage us to ask for what we want, learn to give as well as receive, and affirm that we are whole and lovable just as we are. Because partners are vulnerable to each other, sex also requires trust. You show each other your bodies, with their imperfections. You let go, release, make noise in very private ways.

Since each partner has different moods, rhythms, attitudes, and values about sexuality, it is crucial to discuss sexuality and sexual needs. Both partners can learn about their own sexuality, as well as the sexuality of the other. A key aspect of healthy sexual relating is respect and appreciation. Healthy sexuality is an attitude rather than an act. It involves sexual pleasure, but also soul connection.

Here are some keys to the development of healthy sexual interactions:

1. Let your partner know he or she is beautiful physically, even if he or she doesn't conform to the stereotyped images found in media advertising.
2. Learn your partner's mood and rhythms. Have alternative plans when one of you is not necessarily in the mood for sexual activity.
3. Be flexible, and accommodate your partner.
4. Know what you enjoy, and learn to ask for it.
5. Be patient and considerate of your partner's feelings and body.
6. See sexuality as exploratory rather than only focused on sexual release. Learn to appreciate and know your partner's body. Learn what makes him or her feel wonderful and special.
7. Talk about your feelings, needs, and wants. Share your personal reactions—but remember to be kind.
8. Move beyond labels. See your partner as a wonderful unique human being rather than a male or female. Avoid anti-female or anti-male jokes.
9. Enjoy sexuality as a part of a total relationship. Don't use sex to fix problems or solve arguments.
10. See sexual relating as a chance to enjoy equality—of giving, receiving, and sharing.
11. Don't worry about national averages or whether you are conforming to some norm. Be yourselves.

12. Be playful and have fun.
13. Make sure you have set aside some quiet time away from distractions so you can relax and take time.
14. Teach each other, and learn from each other.
15. Don't expect perfect performance. Be accepting of each other's tiredness or limits.
16. Make sure arousal activities are combined with holding, hugging, and snuggling. Tenderness is the key.
17. Take steps to prevent pregnancy if you do not desire children at this particular time. Share that responsibility equally.
18. Make sure each of you initiates, so that each of you has an opportunity to ask, and each of you has an opportunity to accept.

Brian and Catherine developed a pattern where he was always expected to initiate. As a result, he felt on the spot. He felt that if he didn't initiate sexual activity, it would never happen. He became resentful after a while. When Catherine discovered how he was feeling about it, she agreed to share equally in the responsibility of initiating.

It is important that couples realize that sexual closeness is not the only kind of intimacy they can experience. Emotional connection, spiritual connection, and physical closeness are all ways that support the couple's special sense of we-ness.

MOVING INTO ACTION

1. Which of the eighteen items listed above are most significant for you?

2. What do you enjoy most in a sexual relationship?

3. In what ways do you ask for what you want and need?

4. In what ways do you let your spouse know you want to meet his or her needs?

5. Who initiates and in what ways?

6. What is most enjoyable about the time you spend together? Share these thoughts with your partner.

7. Brainstorm together ways in which your sexual interaction could be more fulfilling for both of you.

8. Plan how you will put one of these ways into action in the coming week.

For this reason a man will leave his father and mother and be joined to his wife, and the two will become one flesh.
—EPHESIANS 5:31

17
AGREEING ON
MONEY MATTERS

Power and money are symbols of manhood, proof of performance,
quick tickets to applause, respect, self-confidence, freedom, and
women for men. Women, while interested in having money, tend to
see it less as an extension of one's self and more as a medium of
exchange. They enjoy the things money can buy.
—CRIS EVATT, HE AND SHE

Many couples argue about money. Money can equal power in a relationship. Whoever earns more may feel entitled to spend more freely. Each of us grew up in a household with certain rules about money. We learned how to save it, how to spend it, how to share it. Two people marrying come from different families and often have different ideas about money. Some families spoke freely to their children about money issues. In other families, children were left totally in the dark about spending and saving. They never knew how much their family had or how decisions were made about purchases or savings. In some families, money was spent easily or even foolishly.

Good healthy marriages involve discussions about money, the value money has in the relationship, and how to spend money fairly. Money must be shared. Attitudes toward money must be agreed upon. Each partner needs to feel like his or her financial contribution is appreciated and valued. There needs to be a common fund for paying bills and discretionary money for each partner to use. You need to agree on how much to spend and how much to save. There needs to be an awareness of how money fits into your spiritual beliefs. For example: How much do you contribute to those in need?

Spiritually, money can be viewed as a necessary evil or an opportunity. Money often determines lifestyle and freedom. In most religions, having money is not the issue. The issue is whether money becomes a god to be worshiped and thereby the major priority of the family. Some people are uncomfortable if they have too much money. They feel guilty about spending money on themselves. Other people believe that money equals happiness—the more you have the better.

Very often, couples learn to compromise about money. Kent and Jean grew up in very different families. Jean's family believed in saving for the future. Purchases were made after careful scrutiny. Her mother would ask her, "Do you really need that? Could we find something almost as good for less money?" Kent's family had more money and spent it more freely. So when Kent and Jean go shopping together, he has a tendency to impulse buy, and she finds that wasteful. They have had several discussions about money and have agreed to compromise. Kent will scout out the purchase possibilities and bring home prices. Then the two of them will discuss alternatives before anything is bought.

Most couples would benefit from a long-range spending plan with some emphasis on retirement. They also need a budget for day-to-day living that includes basic necessities as well as larger purchases (a car, for example). Setting aside time to discuss finances and attitudes towards money is often very helpful. Beliefs about money and how it will be spent need to be part of a couple's spiritual framework.

MOVING INTO ACTION

Some of the basic questions that couples need to address related to money include:

1. How much money do you keep, and how much do you give away?

2. What are life's necessities, and what are the luxuries?

3. What do you really need? What can you do without?

4. Write about your parents' attitudes toward money and how they spent money. Did they agree, disagree?

5. Which attitudes and practices did you adopt because of your parents and which are uniquely your own?

6. In the scheme of things, how important is money in your life?

7. Think about some recent major purchases. How were they made? Who made these purchases?

Discuss these questions with your spouse. Then, examine the ways in which both of you deal with money. Make a list of some of the differences you have regarding spending and saving money.

Come up with a strategy for making money decisions that feels fair to both of you. Work together to create a working budget for day-to-day living. List the major purchases you plan to make in the next year. Discuss how much you will need to save for these purchases. If you need more help, consider contacting a financial adviser you both trust to help you plan for the future.

Keep your lives free from the love of money,
and be content with what you have.
—HEBREWS 13:5

18
SHARING
THE WORK

*They are to do good, to be rich in good works, generous,
and ready to share, thus storing up for themselves the
treasure of a good foundation for the future.*
—1 TIMOTHY 6:18-19

Susan resents the fact that her husband, Roger, never helps around the house. Roger seems oblivious to what needs to be done. After working a full day, Susan comes home and believes that Roger expects her to make the dinner, clean up the mess in the living room, and take out the garbage. Susan is learning to ask Roger for help but wishes he would volunteer so she doesn't have to ask him.

Children grow up in families with different expectations about housework. In some families, everyone helps. In others, the girls help more with the inside-the-house chores and the boys help more with outside chores. In still other families, housekeepers are hired to do the cleaning.

In some families, a person may assume a job will get done without their help or knowledge. Tom has always had clean socks in his drawer, and he has never had to learn to use the washing machine. His mother always did the laundry, and he looked for a wife who would continue that tradition. Jennifer is not happy about his lack of training in this area.

Although household tasks may sound like a trivial issue in becoming soulmates, it is important to create agreed-upon strategies. There is a variety of work to do to keep a household going, much of it tedious and boring. Couples may struggle endlessly about who is to do what and how each one feels about it. A challenge for a healthy relationship is to divide up the chores that need to be done so both people feel the workload is fair.

Household maintenance may not seem like a spiritual experience, but it can be. Having clean clothes, a nice place to live, good food, comfortable resting places, and a furnace that works allows a family to function well. Functioning well can include earning a living, growing personally and spiritually, and contributing to the well-being of others. Examined in this light, household maintenance provides the necessary environment for a family to work for the community's welfare and provides the family with a safe and supportive environment to grow individually and together. If you truly believe the humbled shall be exalted, then you know it is a joy to mop the floor and fold the underwear.

Life involves dust and dirt, messes and the need for cleanup. We need cars that run, food that tastes good, and medical care when we are ill. Accepting maintenance as a necessary part of life may help eliminate complaining. Loving and supportive couples know that there is always much to do around the house.

The challenge is always who does what. In some families, chores are divided by traditional gender roles, and that works fine. In other families, the one who needs the underwear done quickly does the laundry. The one who arrives home first cooks the dinner. The one who has the afternoon off rakes the leaves. Some jobs are more messy than others. Some people may refuse to clean the toilet bowl or cat litter box. Some jobs require higher levels of skill, such as managing investments or doing the taxes. When one spouse works fifty or more hours outside the home, the other spouse who works less might pick up more of the household chores.

There are the daily maintenance jobs, the monthly jobs, and the yearly jobs. Couples need to discuss each job, its requirements, who is more capable of handling it, and ways of dividing chores so it feels fair to both people. One large monthly job might mean that the other spouse do more of the daily work.

If you have children, enlisting their help is important. They also need to learn about the amount of work it takes to run a household. They need to develop maintenance skills so they won't become helpless or dependent on their own spouse to do everything for them.

Some couples rotate chores for variety. After doing the cooking for ten years, Marjorie decided that it was Frank's turn. But she had to let go of her idea of the perfectly well-balanced meal, as Frank's idea of cooking was simpler than hers.

No two couples are alike, and the way chores are divided should reflect a couple's skills, interests, time, and particular lifestyle. But you can be sure that settling this issue helps a couple move to a happier level of functioning. Doing the chores efficiently allows both partners to move on to spending more quality time in other ways. Some chores can be done together and can add to a feeling a closeness and teamwork.

MOVING INTO ACTION

Make a list of everything around your house or apartment that needs to get done. Chores include chauffeuring children, washing dishes, cooking meals, shopping, doing laundry, paying bills, vacuuming, dusting, emptying the garbage, recycling, taking care of pets, putting up storm windows and screens, gardening, etc. Don't forget the more invisible jobs like dealing with insurance companies or planning social activities.

List the jobs that are the main priorities and those that are not. List those that need to be done daily, weekly, monthly, yearly.

Rate each job by its desirability. Least liked jobs receive three points. Somewhat liked jobs receive two points, and really enjoyable jobs receive one point. When you choose jobs with your spouse, add up your number of points and see how equal your scores are.

Discuss with each other your attitudes about household maintenance. Then ask yourself the following:

1. Who does what, and how has that been decided?

2. How do you each feel about the kinds and amount of work you do?

3. Is either of you doing too much or feeling taken for granted?

4. What can be done if that is the case?

5. How do you show appreciation for jobs well done?

6. How do you trade jobs?

7. If you have children, how are they involved in household maintenance?

8. Can you develop any strategies for making household chores more fun?

So I saw that there is nothing better than that all should enjoy their work.
—ECCLESIATES 3:22

19
COPING WITH KIDS

Children: The Challenge
BOOK TITLE BY RUDOLPH DREIKURS

The birth of a child is an exciting and miraculous event. For some parents who are unprepared for the stresses and demands of an infant, a birth can create rifts between a father and a mother. Raising children takes commitment and maturity. Soulmates do much better at parenting than a couple who are at a stalemate with each other. Soulmates are able to share concerns, doubts, and goals—and can therefore work out a loving way to raise children.

Even if you don't have biological children of your own, you will probably be relating to nieces and nephews, godchildren, children in your care from Big Brother/Big Sister organizations, or friends' children.

Thousands of books are written about parenting, and many of them are extremely helpful. Here, we will discuss issues related to discipline, which seem to be the ones about which couples most often disagree.

We are all raised with different styles of discipline. Some parents punished us with time outs, others with guilt, and still others with harsh words. Some used spankings. The key to developing healthy discipline for children is to agree upon a style of discipline, and stick to it. Children know how to wedge in between parents when they disagree about discipline. They go to the most lenient parent first. The best way around this is for parents to form a united front when it comes to discipline.

Children often test our limits. It is important for the couple to have an agreed upon belief system about discipline and a coherent style. Parents need to know what the limits are and why they are the limits. It is also helpful for each parent to know what bothers the other parent most. Then, each can take over when the other seems to lose patience and coping ability.

Children require structure. They are most helped by parents who act competently, consistently, and maturely. They do best when adults around them do not threaten, shame or ridicule them—but try to teach them the acceptable ways to behave in a variety of situations and the logical consequences that come from misbehaving.

Children model their behavior after the adults in their lives. Children also learn a great deal from watching grown-ups. It is important for adults to model healthy communication skills and healthy habits. What irritates you in your spouse is likely to be the same behavior you observe in your child. And then children may say when they are criticized, "Well, Daddy acts like that so why can't I?"

Children need explanations about why certain behaviors are unacceptable. It is helpful if spouses can verbalize to each other the range of acceptable and unacceptable behaviors in private and the reasons behaviors fall into these two categories. Clear, concise reasoning can help children understand that parents are not just being critical—they have good reasons for requiring the behaviors they set for their children.

Consistency is very important. It is vital that parents not only agree upon a discipline style, but also act consistently to reinforce it. This works best if parents are not overtired or overstressed when coping with misbehavior.

Both parents need to share the disciplinary role. It is helpful if mom does not say, "Wait until your father comes home." Children need to learn that both parents are adults and can enforce family rules.

MOVING INTO ACTION

Identify a specific situation in which your child misbehaves. Discuss your disciplinary strategy.

1. What do you expect from your children at different ages?

2. Do you equally share the disciplinary role? If not, what roles do you and your spouse play?

3. If you disagree on discipline, how can you work together to compromise on a particular strategy?

Train children in the right way,
and when old, they will not stray.
—PROVERBS 22:6

20
RESPECTING EACH
OTHER'S FAMILY

He wants me to call him "Dad." I already have a Dad,
and don't want another one. I don't want to hurt his feelings,
but I am not comfortable calling Joe "Dad."
—A SON-IN-LAW

Mike and Marilyn used to argue a lot about her family.
Mike didn't especially like Marilyn's father and believed he
didn't treat her mother well. Marilyn found herself defend-
ing her father and feeling resentful for having to do so. After
talking about it together, Marilyn encouraged Mike to
accept her father as he was. Mike convinced Marilyn that he
would be willing to do that if he didn't have to spend hours
and hours with him. So, when Marilyn's folks come over for
dinner, Mike visits over dinner and then excuses himself and
leaves. Marilyn covers for Mike saying he has work to do in
his study.

It is said that when you marry someone, you also marry
their whole family. In some ways, the family of origin is
already inside your partner. But even if not, you will have to
deal with the unique and idiosyncratic ways of your extended
family. In-laws can feel like outlaws at times.

Families differ from each other, and members have unique
ways of dealing with time, crises, money, holidays, illnesses,
relationships, conflicts, food, shopping, and vacations. It is
rare that a person likes everything about his or her own family, let alone a spouse's family. So how do you deal with these
special people? Very gingerly.

It is important to remember that although you may not like certain aspects of your partner's family, they are still family. People frequently become defensive when they believe their family is being criticized by others while in fact they may feel the same way about them themselves.

In a healthy relationship, partners support each other's attachment to their family as long as that family does not intrude or try to disrupt the couple's relationship. Having firm boundaries in the marriage means that in-laws are not necessarily aware of personal or intimate details about the relationship. Individuals who use their parents to complain about their partner are inviting difficult spouse-in-law interactions.

Each partner needs to affirm the other's involvement in activities with their parents, but clear limits and boundaries about how often they will see their parents must be set. There are occasions when it makes sense for one's partner to visit his or her family on their own. It is helpful for both of you to discuss how you feel about the other spending time alone with their own family.

In some cases, a spouse may even be closer to his or her in-laws than to his or her own family. This too brings up issues that can be discussed between partners.

It is also important not to bring up in-law issues when you are having a disagreement about something else. Your partner may share personality traits with his or her parents, and some of them may be upsetting to you. It is important to focus on your partner, not your in-laws.

Another significant issue is parental illness. As parents age and become ill or limited in their capabilities, partners should have an honest discussion about how much responsibility they will take for their own parents. Some people feel it is their duty to let an aging parent move in with them. This should be carefully discussed in advance. You both might agree to such an arrangement in advance but when the time comes find it impossible to live with an aging in-law. It is important to maintain flexibility and allow for a change of mind by either partner.

The challenge is that we may feel a primary allegiance to our partner and also a very strong desire to help our aging parents. There are no right or wrong answers when this situation occurs. Couples need to be flexible and open-minded, as well as willing to be clear about their own limits and preferences.

MOVING INTO ACTION

Make a list of some of the important issues regarding in-laws. Here are a few questions for you to consider as you write:

1. How close do you feel toward your own family?

2. How close do you feel toward your spouse's family?

3. How much time do you wish to spend with your own family?

4. How much time do you wish to spend with your spouse's family?

5. How does your spouse feel about your family involvement?

6. What kind of commitment do you have toward your family as they age?

7. What is the most difficult aspect in visiting your family?

8. What is the most difficult aspect in visiting your spouse's family?

9. What boundaries and limits do both you and your spouse need to set regarding extended family?

Identify one problem that distresses you most as you think about your in-laws. Brainstorm some possible strategies for coping with this problem. Consider how much time you wish to spend with them and ways of compromising with your spouse about your involvement.

Grandchildren are the crown of the aged,
and the glory of children is their parents.
—PROVERBS 17:6

ENHANCING THE
SPIRITUAL JOURNEY

21
SHARING A
SPIRITUAL JOURNEY

*Over and over again God calls you and me to the gardening of our
own divine depths, to the cultivation of what is called the true seed
within us. God calls us to tend what lies seeded in the soul, this
kernel of our truest nature—the God-image or True Self.*
—SUE MONK KIDD, *WHEN THE HEART WAITS*

Partnership is strongest when both partners share a strong faith. This means a faith in God, in themselves, in life, in their future. Although each person must make the spiritual journey on his or her own, it is wonderful if spouses can share it together. The faith journey involves our relationship with God, principles of peace and social justice, protecting the ecological balance, and compassion toward all people. What is vital is that each partner nurture the other along that faith journey, giving support and encouragement each step of the way. Some of the basic ideas that might be helpful include:

1. God loves us for who we are. We don't have to prove anything. This is the real love, the true love. It is magnificent, overwhelming, incomprehensible.
2. God forgives us in advance and accepts our limitations. God knows us inside out and doesn't expect perfection, only humility. When we falter or fail, God is there to catch us.
3. We can never be abandoned by God. Even though we have felt abandoned by people and know the pain of loss, betrayal, and disappointment, God stands by us.

4. We must be still to hear God. We need to slow down, pray, meditate, confess. It is in the quiet that God's voice becomes clearer to us.

5. Fear keeps us stuck. Fear blocks God's love for us. God will give us our daily bread.

6. What we believe we want may not be what we need. We are limited in our ability to know what is always best for us. Sometimes things come our way which seem to make little sense. What seem like curses can turn into blessings. We don't always get the true picture right away.

7. We are all on a journey. No one has arrived. Every journey is unique and yet every journey is ultimately the same. Everyone is seeking God. There is a God-sized hole in every human heart.

8. We already have a taste of eternity. Spiritual life on earth is like heaven. If we know God, we don't expect people to be God. We don't expect things to take the place of God.

9. Life is a never-ending opportunity to see the good. We can turn hardship into hope. Spirituality is about seeing things differently, through God's eyes.

10. We must try to forgive people and the world for its limits. Anger keeps us stuck in the past.

11. Although we must have an ego, a sense of self, we also must focus on spirit and let ego take a secondary role.

12. Spirituality is about seeing the sacred in the ordinary, paying attention, and noticing the wonder of creation.

13. Our ultimate goal is compassionate love.

14. Loving attachment does not die. Death is not the victor—love is. When someone we love dies, we can still feel their presence inside of us.

15. To transform the world, we have to transform ourselves. Spiritual transformation creates miracles.

16. Serenity comes from trusting the process. We must act as if everything depended upon us and pray as if everything depended on God.

17. We should have the innocence of children, the discernment of adults, and the trust of infants in order to live spiritually in the world. We need to be cautious, but not cynical. We need to have hope, but not be easily fooled.

18. The process of growth is one of purification. We gain things and lose things. Life is a matter of reaching out and letting go. Relax into your destiny. It will be all right.

19. Life is about learning, not achieving. Every experience is an opportunity to learn. Every experience we encounter gives us the chance to say yes to God. When we falter and fail, we learn something about ourselves. God will not fail to pick us up.

20. What is most significant is often invisible to us. Hope, faith, and love keep things going. When it looks like nothing is happening, God is quietly at work.

21. God is patient, always waiting for us to catch on.

Many of you are already on a spiritual journey. It is important that both of you support each other's journey. Encourage each other to continue to grow spiritually, to continue to connect with God, to read the Bible, to pray, to meditate, to commune with nature, to journal, to go on spiritual retreats.

The challenge of sharing a spiritual journey is that two people often have different ideas about their spirituality. One might feel an affinity for a particular religious institution and the other may not. If you are of different traditions, try to learn about each other's and possibly incorporate some of them into your own journey. While your ideas may differ, it is important to realize that ultimately all spiritual journeys bring us closer to God, closer to ourselves, and closer to others.

MOVING INTO ACTION

Spirituality requires ongoing dialogue. As you read the twenty-one points above, which seem most powerful or helpful with regard to your own journey? Discuss what some of these mean to you with your spouse.

Share some meaningful time together experiencing your spirituality—go for a walk, pray, sing, attend church.

Grow in grace and in the knowledge of our Lord Jesus Christ.
—2 PETER 3:18

22
THE ART OF
FORGIVING

Forgiveness is the act of admitting we are like other people.
We are prone to make mistakes that cause confusion, inflict pain,
and miscommunicate our intentions. We are the recipients of these
human errors and the perpetrators. There is no way we can avoid
hurting others or being hurt by others, because this is exactly
the nature of our imperfection. The only choice we have
is to reconcile ourselves to our own flaws and the flaws of
other people, or withdraw from the community.
—CHRISTINA BALDWIN, *LIFE'S COMPANION*

Forgiveness needs to be part of our healing repertoire. We need to forgive ourselves because it is too painful to live with self-hatred. We need to forgive those we love because grudges get in the way of intimate connecting. Holding onto grudges limits our ability to love ourselves, our partner, and life itself. Grudges create a one-up, one-down relationship that creates animosity and inequality.

Forgiveness is a spiritual practice that comes from God's grace—God's unending ability to love us despite our problems, limits, and mistakes. One way that some people enable themselves to forgive is by experiencing God's grace on an ongoing basis. Knowing that they are forgiven grants them the motivation and generosity to forgive others. The art of forgiveness is not just a one-time behavior; it is a spiritual attitude.

Grudges keep us stuck in the past. As prisoners of our past, we may hang onto them as a way of making ourselves feel important, self-righteous, superior, or in control. Forgiving involves an acceptance of our own limits and brokenness and our separation from God. Forgiveness is accepting your spouse for who your spouse is, and loving him or her anyway.

Peter and Diane have a difficult time letting go of past hurts. Whenever they engage in arguments, Peter brings up remarks that Diane made to him ten years ago. Diane becomes angry and defensive. Peter becomes angry at Diane's defensiveness. Both of them need to learn to break this pattern because it inflicts additional pain on their marriage.

It is, of course, more difficult to forgive someone who intentionally hurts us. We tend to take the attack very personally and feel threatened. When intentional hurt occurs, partners need to share how they feel about it as soon as they are aware of it. People usually hurt others out of their own suffering and pain. Sometimes people speak in the heat of the moment, and in anger, vent in cruel and hurtful ways.

In developing a forgiving attitude, it is important to accept your own limitations. Some people have a difficult time forgiving themselves for their own imperfections and then become critical of others as well. Think about what you are going to say to your spouse before you say it, and try to imagine the effect it will have on your partner.

Forgiveness is also related to the idea of seeing the "big picture." When you understand that you are a part of another person's life for forty or fifty years, little incidents and remarks take on less significance. You can let them go and not take them personally because, in the long run, it doesn't matter. We need to learn that relationships will inevitably have their moments of hurt, of sadness, of loss, and of fear. These are all part of life. We can't avoid being hurt and hurting others as we journey along our path. However, we can become more careful about what we say and how we say it. We can become more loving and forgiving as we go.

Developing your forgiving attitude requires a deeper connection with God. This can happen through prayer, through journaling, through meditation, through reading the Bible. Knowing God's love and grace can give a sense of peace to your life and result in less self-righteousness and need to judge and condemn others.

Forgiveness is a spiritual practice; it releases us from the past, so we can move forward toward the future with love and confidence.

MOVING INTO ACTION

Think about the grudges you may be carrying around. Write them down. Find someone against whom you are holding a grudge and tell them you forgive them. Apologize to someone you have hurt.

Ask your spouse if there is some hurt which you inflicted that you can apologize for. Exchange letters of forgiveness with each other.

Examine your relationship to God's grace. Make a list of your limits and weaknesses knowing that they are forgiven by God.

1. In what ways are you affected by God's forgiveness for your sins?

2. How does that forgiveness manifest itself in your ability to forgive others?

Be kind to one another, tenderhearted, forgiving one another,
as God in Christ has forgiven you.
—EPHESIANS 4:32

23
CELEBRATING
TOGETHER

*Ritual consists of the external practices of spirituality
that help us become more receptive and aware of the
closeness of our lives to the sacred. Ritual is the act
of sanctifying action so that it has meaning.*
—CHRISTINA BALDWIN, *LIFE'S COMPANION*

Families are helped by rituals, traditions, and celebrations. These give meaning to our lives. We go through transitions and need to mark passages. We experience losses that require rituals. We develop traditions linking us with our past, celebrating our present, and leading us onward to the future. Through family traditions, couples can gain a sense of personal meaning, spiritual connectedness, and family identity.

Holidays are marked with certain celebrations. Graduations, birthdays, and anniversaries can be celebrated in ways that link family members together and strengthen the couple bond. As couples celebrate, they can document their rituals and pass these on to future generations.

Mealtimes and other daily practices can provide opportunity to connect spiritually as well as personally. The major life cycle rituals and transitions can be celebrated with parties, dinners, music, or readings. There are traditions that involve beginnings and endings. Rituals also provide us with healing experiences when we have experienced a loss, betrayal, or disappointment.

In an article called "Rituals for Our Times," Evan Imber-Black and Janine Roberts state that "the truly magical quality of rituals is embedded in their capacity not only to announce a change but to actually create the change. Change is *enacted* through rituals and not simply talked about."

Individuals hunger for meaning and connectedness. Symbols and rituals can connect us with each other and God in meaningful ways. It is possible to create ceremonies that celebrate milestones in your life. It is possible to create new traditions that reinforce a couple's uniqueness. Special stories can be told and written which commemorate lives and important events.

Sally and James have developed several family rituals which they practice on a regular basis. They celebrate each of their children's birthdays by having the child select the dinner menu. That child's chores are done by others on their birthday. They also have a bedtime ritual in which each child prays with their parents for their friends, family members, or even strangers. A family ritual might include a service for a pet that died. A ritual might even occur each night as a prayer before eating dinner.

MOVING INTO ACTION

Think of family rituals and traditions you grew up with. Make a list. Together, think of new rituals and traditions you have created as a couple.

1. Begin a "milestone book" where you keep track of changes that have occurred in your life—weddings, birthdays, confirmations, school plays, concerts, athletic championships, anniversaries, family vacations, job promotions, friendships, and other changes. These can all be photographed and kept together.

2. Create one new ritual or tradition together that you could practice as a family. Think of some special activity that has personal meaning for you and your spouse.

It could be a special prayer, ceremony, or event which marks a transition. It could be a craft that the family works on together. It could be something you do around dinnertime, or bedtime, or on weekends.

Rejoice always, pray without ceasing, give thanks in all circumstances, for this is the will of God in Christ Jesus for you.
—1 THESSALONIANS 5:16

24
SPIRITUALITY MAKES A BETTER MARRIAGE

A soul connection is a resonance between two people who respond to the essential beauty of each other's individual natures, behind their facades, and who connect on this deeper level. This kind of mutual recognition provides the catalyst for a potent alchemy. It is a sacred alliance whose purpose is to help both partners discover and realize their deepest potentials. While a heart connection lets us appreciate those we love just as they are, a soul connection opens up a further dimension—seeing and loving them for who they could be, and for who we could become under their influence.
—JOHN WELWOOD, *LOVE AND AWAKENING*

When I look around at couples who communicate well, share joy, and have a deep commitment to each other, I discover that many of these couples share a strong spiritual lifestyle. Often, I see these couples sing together, work together, and pray together. I am beginning to understand that a deep commitment to one's spirituality makes a person a better marriage partner. What are the qualities of deep spirituality, and how do they lend themselves to a healthier marriage?

1. Spirituality relates to humility. Spiritual people know they are not God. They can admit their mistakes and don't have to be right all the time. They are willing to compromise, share work, and negotiate. They don't

try to control others and are willing to surrender to a higher purpose.

2. Spiritual people are compassionate. People who believe in the unity of all of creation believe that other people's feelings are as important as their own. Therefore, in marriage, spirituality leads to empathy, concern for others, and a commitment that goes beyond oneself.

3. They experience joy in being alive. While there is an acknowledgment of pain and suffering, spiritually-oriented people see the joy in everyday experiences. They understand that pain and suffering are not the last words.

4. Spiritually-focused people have hope. Along with joy, they believe that good can come out of evil and they have hope in the future.

5. Spiritual people know how to forgive. Experiencing God's gift of grace and forgiveness, spiritual people don't expect perfection from others. They can accept the human limitations of their partner.

6. They are not totally dependent on their partner. Since spiritually-oriented people have something greater than people as the cornerstone of their lives, namely God, they don't rely on their partner to give them everything. They know God loves them for who they are and, therefore, don't feel empty and needy all the time.

7. They develop discernment, and when they trust, they trust completely. Spiritual discernment teaches the difference between words and deeds. Those who are spiritually committed learn to recognize those who are trustworthy and then trust them with their whole heart.

8. Spiritually oriented people have self-discipline and a feeling of accountability. Focusing on spirituality

requires commitment, discipline and being responsible for the consequences of one's own actions. This leads to emotional maturity in relationships.

9. Spiritual people realize that life is a journey, and see themselves in process. Because of this, they understand how people can grow from suffering and adversity. They don't expect to be perfect for their partner or for their partner to be perfect. They tend to see the larger picture.

10. Spiritual people know how to love. Since the essence of spirituality is about loving, spiritual people try to turn fear into love. They love God, themselves, others, and the earth. They develop a loving attitude, which means they are not infatuated with love, but they see the relationship between love, work, and responsibility.

11. They don't need things to make them happy. Those who focus on their spiritual growth know they can't buy happiness in a store. They are not insatiable and do not try to fill themselves up by having the latest fashions or inventions. As a result, they focus on the meaning of life rather than on possessions.

12. They know how to celebrate. Since ritual and celebration is such an important part of spiritual life, those who focus on their spiritual growth enjoy celebrating the special times as well as everyday events—such as a sunrise. This leads to an appreciation of all of life's gifts, and they celebrate with joy all family events.

These qualities contribute to a depth of understanding that nurtures the spiritual journey of both partners. Instead of looking lovingly only into their partner's eyes, spiritual people hold hands and look lovingly out into the world.

MOVING INTO ACTION

Let each partner choose the three qualities of a deep spirituality that are most significant for him or her.

Share your responses and discuss how these qualities could contribute to the health of your marriage.

I pray that, according to the riches of his glory, he may grant that you may be strengthened in your inner being with power through his Spirit, and that Christ may dwell in your hearts through faith, as you are being rooted and grounded in love.
—EPHESIANS 3:16-17

INTO THE FUTURE

25
WHERE DO WE GO FROM HERE?

Congratulations! You have read the chapters, done the exercises, attempted the questions. You have examined who you are, what you want, how you view God, how you wish to live. Most couples have not done as thorough a job as you have.

What I hope you have discovered as you have taken this journey is that growing individually and growing together takes time, energy, work, and commitment. Without those, nothing much happens.

Marriage is a remarkable teacher. Marriage partners often hold mirrors up to our faces. We can see things about ourselves that we both like and dislike. If you have discovered some issues which are too difficult for you to handle by yourselves, you might consider counseling with a therapist or pastor. While many couples can work out interpersonal and spiritual differences by themselves, some require professional help and support to continue to grow in love and faith.

Your marriage is like a plant. Couples are either growing or dying. I hope you choose to continually grow and blossom. Fruits will come of your labors, because you will appreciate each other, know God, and trust the process.

Continue to keep the lines of communication open. Continue to experience God's love, in whatever ways work for you. Meditate, pray, sing, laugh, dance, confess, join in social groups that encourage healthy growth. But also, take time out to rest, relax, and be still. Be active and be silent. Be nurturing and be loving. Most of all, celebrate who you are as individuals and who you are as a couple. As children of God, you have potential beyond compare!

BIBLIOGRAPHY

Baldwin, Christina. *Life's Companion*. New York: Bantam, 1990.

Bozarth, Alla. *Life Is Goodbye, Life Is Hello*. Minneapolis, MN: Comp-Care Publications, 1982.

Bugen, Larry A. *Love and Renewal*. Oakland, CA: New Harbinger, 1990.

Carr, Jacquelyn B. *Crisis In Intimacy*. Pacific Grove, CA: Brooks/Cole, 1988.

Covey, Stephen R. *Principle-Centered Leadership*. New York: Simon and Schuster, 1990.

Dreikurs, Rudolph. *Children the Challenge*. New York: Duell, Sloan & Pearce, 1964.

Erdahl, Lowell and Carol. *Be Good to Each Other*. Minneapolis: Augsburg Fortress Publishers, 1991. 96 pages.

Evatt, Cris. *He and She: 60 Significant Differences Between Men and Women*. Berkeley, CA: Conari Press, 1992.

Gray, John. *Women Are from Venus, Men Are from Mars*. New York: HarperCollins, 1992.

Hendrix, Harville. *Getting the Love You Want*. New York: Holt, 1988.

Jampolsky, Gerald. *Love Is Letting Go of Fear*. Millbrae, CA: Celestial Arts, 1979.

Kidd, Sue Monk. *When the Heart Waits*. San Francisco: HarperSanFrancisco, 1992.

Oates, Wayne E. *Nurturing Silence in a Noisy Heart*. Minneapolis: Augsburg Fortress Publishers, 1996.

Paul, Jordan and Margaret. *Do I Have to Give Up Me To Be Loved By You?* Minneapolis: CompCare Publishers, 1983.

Smedes, Lewis B. *Caring and Commitment*. San Francisco: Harper & Row, 1988.

Storr, Anthony. *Solitude*. New York: Free Press, 1988.

Tannen, Deborah. *You Just Don't Understand*. New York: Morrow, 1990.

Viorst, Judith. *Necessary Losses*. New York: Ballantine, 1986.

Welwood, John. *Journey of the Heart*. New York: HarperCollins, 1990.

Wicks, Robert J. *Living Simply In an Anxious World*. Mahwah, NJ: Paulist Press, 1988.

Williamson, Marianne. *A Return to Love*. New York: HarperCollins, 1992.